Melly Xmas

Habby

from Wifie XX.

Mite Hetmill

SAFC.

XY

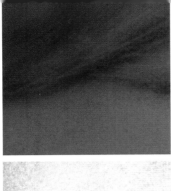

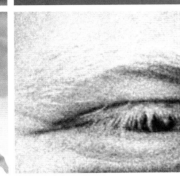

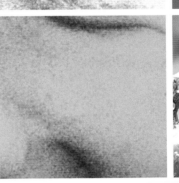

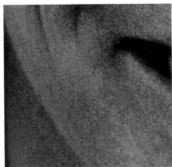
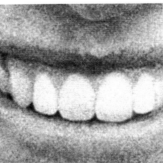

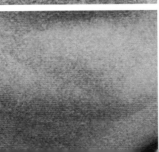

MICKY'S
TOP FIFTY

SUNDERLAND AFC PLAYERS OF HIS GENERATION

Written by Micky Horswill and Brian Leng

A TWOCAN PUBLICATION

©2015. Published by twocan.

ISBN: 978-1-909872-75-2

PICTURES: Action Images, Mirrorpix, North East Press, Press Association.

IN MEMORY OF A SUPPORTER AND A FRIEND

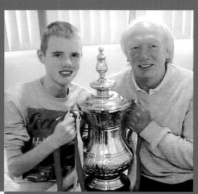

I would like to dedicate this book to a massive Sunderland fan that I had the pleasure of getting to know and was able to call a friend.

I met this remarkable young man when he asked if I could spare the time to meet him and sign his beloved 1973 Cup Final Shirt, which I did, after which we kept in touch on Facebook and became good friends.

A while later after hearing he was ill in hospital and paying him a visit, I was both saddened and shocked to discover that his infectious sense of humour hid a battle he had never mentioned.

On 6 March 2015 aged only 24, he lost his fight against Cystic Fibrosis, but as ill as he was he never lost his spirit and the courage he showed for life.

His name was Chris Wright, a lovely person who will never be forgotten by anyone who knew or met him.

God Bless My Good Friend

3

CONTENTS

06 FOREWORD	64 JIMMY McNAB
08 JULIO ARCA	66 JIMMY MONTGOMERY
10 GORDON ARMSTRONG	68 GEORGE MULHALL
12 LEN ASHURST	70 RICHARD ORD
14 JOE BAKER	72 GARY OWERS
16 KEVIN BALL	74 KEVIN PHILLIPS
18 JIM BAXTER	76 NICK PICKERING
20 GARY BENNETT	78 RITCHIE PITT
22 JOE BOLTON	80 IAN PORTERFIELD
24 PAUL BRACEWELL	82 NIALL QUINN
26 JODY CRADDOCK	84 BRYAN ROBSON
28 JOHNNY CROSSAN	86 DANNY ROSE
30 SHAUN ELLIOTT	88 GARY ROWELL
32 MARCO GABBIADINI	90 NICK SHARKEY
34 ERIC GATES	92 THOMAS SORENSEN
36 MICHAEL GRAY	94 COLIN SUGGETT
38 RON GUTHRIE	96 COLIN TODD
40 VIC HALOM	98 DENNIS TUEART
42 GORDON HARRIS	100 CHRIS TURNER
44 MARTIN HARVEY	102 BARRY VENISON
46 GEORGE HERD	104 DAVE WATSON
48 BILLY HUGHES	106 BILLY WHITEHURST
50 CHARLIE HURLEY	
52 CECIL IRWIN	
54 KENWYNE JONES	
56 BOBBY KERR	
58 SEBASTIAN LARSSON	
60 DICK MALONE	
62 NEIL MARTIN	

FOREWORD

When I was first asked to produce a book on my Fifty Greatest Sunderland Players, I quickly realised that the dilemma I faced was not who to include, but who to leave out! There were so many great players on my original list of possibles, that arriving at the final fifty really did become a truly daunting task.

The parameters for the book were simply to include only players I had actually seen perform as a supporter on the terraces together with those I actually played alongside during my own Roker Park career.

My earliest memory of supporting Sunderland was during the 1963/64 promotion season and many of the players from that team are included, whereas other greats such as Stan Anderson, Brian Clough and Len Shackleton miss out, simply because I never saw them play. Not surprisingly, many of my former Roker Park colleagues are featured, including all of the 1973 FA Cup-winning team - how could I leave out any of the team that produced arguably the greatest victory in the history of the competition!

Selecting the finest or greatest players from any club is an impossible task which will always produce an endless debate, as every supporter will always have their own personal view on who should be included. I'm sure one or two of the players in my selection will raise a few eyebrows, but surely that is what makes football so great, it's all about opinions - I hope you enjoy.

Micky Horswill

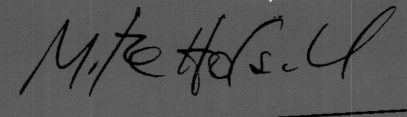

JULIO ARCA

Signed by Sunderland manager Peter Reid in the summer of 2000, Julio Arca made an immediate impact by scoring on his debut to secure a 1-1 draw against West Ham United. Reid had spotted the Argentinian left-back in an Under-21s match against England at Craven Cottage and had to hold off stiff competition from a number of Premier League clubs, including Newcastle United and Leeds United. Eventually, it took a £3.5 million fee to land the Argentinos Juniors star, but it was soon clear that the Sunderland boss had landed a real gem.

Converted to a left-sided midfielder by Reid, Julio soon became a great favourite with Black Cats' fans and he capped an outstanding first season on Wearside by returning home to captain the Argentina team that won the FIFA Under-20 World Cup tournament in Buenos Aires.

The peak of his Sunderland career was probably 2004 when he was voted Player of the Year and was a key member of Mick McCarthy's Football League Championship-winning side of 2004/05. Sadly, relegation a year later brought an end to Julio's career at the Stadium of Light when he was sold to Middlesbrough for a fee of £1.75 million. These days he is back living in Sunderland and whilst his top-class career finally came to an end in 2011, he still turns out regularly for South Shields in the Northern League.

"Julio came as an attacking left-back and soon showed his qualities both in defending and even more so in his attacking play.

"He had an excellent left foot and loved to get forward and produce telling crosses for his strikers, so much so that Peter Reid moved him forward to play as an attacking wide midfielder where he became very successful. He also showed a passion to win and always gave his all in every game he played."

Micky

GORDON ARMSTRONG

An outstanding midfielder with an eye for goal, Gordon was only 17 when he was handed his Sunderland debut in a Division One game against West Bromwich Albion at the Hawthorns towards the end of the 1984/85 season.

It was the start of a lengthy career at Roker Park that would see the Newcastle-born youngster pick up two Young Player of the Year awards before going on to clock up over 400 appearances for the club, a record that earned him a place in the list of Sunderland's top ten all-time appearance makers.

Gordon was a key player in the Sunderland team that lifted the Third Division championship in 1988 and then won promotion back to the top flight two years later. A regular goal-scorer for the club, Gordon possessed exceptional aerial ability and Sunderland fans will no doubt remember his dramatic late winner against Chelsea in the 1992 FA Cup quarter-final replay at Roker Park. He picked up a losers medal in the final against Liverpool at Wembley that year and eventually went on to net 61 goals for Sunderland, before his career on Wearside came to a close during the 1996 close-season.

Gordon then joined Bury before moving on to Burnley where he enjoyed five seasons with the Turf Moor club before retiring from the game in 2003.

"A favourite of mine, Gordon was, in my view, a greatly under-rated player who never let us down.

"He was a power-house in the middle of the park, who was very energetic getting all over the pitch from box to box as well as having a habit of getting into the opposition penalty area to get on the end of crosses and score lots of goals. Now living locally, Gordon is still in the game and is part of our Former Players' golf squad, where he is a bandit!"

Micky

11

LEN ASHURST

A terrific servant for Sunderland, Merseyside-born Len Ashurst was signed from local club Prescot Cables in December 1957, having previously been on Liverpool's books for the best part of four years. An England Youth international, Len was handed his debut by Sunderland manager Alan Brown early in the 1958/59 season as the Sunderland boss began a rebuilding programme following his team's relegation to Division Two the season before.

Thereafter, Len quickly became established as the club's regular left-back, soon earning a reputation as an uncompromising, tough-tackling defender and in 1961, he was capped by England at Under-23 level. A consistent performer who rarely missed a game, Len was an ever-present in the 1963/64 season when promotion back to the top flight was finally achieved.

His career at Roker Park finally came to an end in March 1971 after making 452 appearances for Sunderland, a record only bettered by Jimmy Montgomery and his loyalty was rewarded with a testimonial match against Newcastle United at Roker Park. Len then joined Hartlepool United as player-manager on a free transfer, before taking charge at Sheffield Wednesday, followed by a great spell in Wales taking both Newport County and Cardiff City into Europe. In 1984 he made a sentimental return to Wearside to take over the Roker Park hot-seat and whilst he took the club to the Milk Cup final in his first season, relegation followed soon after the Wembley defeat against Norwich City and he parted ways with the club. These days Len lives in Whitburn and is still involved in the game working for the FA Premier League as a Match Delegate.

"The left-back who was the final part of the 60s back four. A hard hitting full-back who was as steady as anyone that played for Sunderland, Len was nicknamed 'The Lion' for his ferocious tackling and big heart.

"The highest compliment I can pay Len is that the late, great George Best said the two hardest full-backs he ever played against were Paul Reaney of Leeds United and Len Ashurst of Sunderland - WOW!"

Micky

13

JOE BAKER

A prolific goal-scorer with Aberdeen, Joe Baker was one of the hottest properties around in Scottish football during the 1950s and whilst there is no question he was a Scotsman through and through, Joe was actually born in Liverpool. That fact had not gone unnoticed with the England selectors and international honours soon followed for Joe, first with the Under-23 team and then at full international level.

A move to a bigger club was inevitable and in May 1961, he moved out to Italy to join AC Torino along with another talented Scot, Denis Law of Manchester City. However, both players found it difficult in the negative Italian League and soon returned home, Joe joining Arsenal in a £67,000 transfer, while Denis returned to Manchester to join United. Joe spent almost four years at Highbury, his quick and skilful attacking play making him a great favourite on the terraces, before moving on to join Nottingham Forest midway through the 1965/66 season.

It was in June 1969, just before his 29th birthday that Joe arrived at Roker Park following a £30,000 transfer and whilst his best years may well have been behind him, the qualities that had established him as one of English football's finest strikers were still there for all to see.

A hugely popular player, who always played the game with real enthusiasm, Joe was a great favourite with Sunderland fans and also with his colleagues in the dressing room. His stay with Sunderland lasted little more than eighteen months before he headed back north of the border to join Hibernian and he will probably be best remembered at Roker Park for a brilliant hat-trick he scored against Charlton Athletic early in the 1970/71 season.

Joe then played for Raith Rovers and had two spells managing Albion Rovers before retiring from the game and moving into the pub trade. He died in October 2003 at the age of 63 after suffering a heart attack during a charity golf tournament.

"A right character, Joe was at the club when I joined as an apprentice in 1969. I would often watch him in training and at times I used to wonder just how he managed to get into our first team, but come matchday Joe would show everyone what a great player he really was.

"Reading the game so well, he would get into positions other people never thought of and after receiving the ball he then showed what a great finisher he was."
Micky

KEVIN BALL

Born in Hastings, Kevin began his professional career with Portsmouth and after making his debut in January 1984 he helped Pompey win promotion from Division Two in 1987. He joined Sunderland in a £350,000 transfer in July 1990, shortly after the Roker Park club had won promotion back to the top flight and in the years ahead his inspirational play and never-say-die approach would establish him as a real cult figure with the fans.

Initially used as a central defender alongside Gary Bennett, Kevin picked up the Player of the Year award in his first season on Wearside before being moved into a central midfield role where his tough-tackling and ball-winning ability quickly established him as one the games toughest characters. His strong leadership qualities both on and off the pitch eventually saw Kevin take over as team captain, a role he held throughout the remainder of his Sunderland career.

After appearing in the 1992 FA Cup final against Liverpool, Kevin went on to lead Sunderland to two Division One championships in 1996 and 1999, eventually making 388 appearances for the club and scoring 27 goals. His loyalty was rewarded with a testimonial match against Sampdoria in July 1999 and a few months later, he joined Fulham in a £200,000 transfer. Kevin later had a spell with Burnley before returning to the Stadium of Light in a coaching capacity at the club's academy and he twice briefly held the post of caretaker-manager when Mick McCarthy and Paolo Di Canio left the club. Still involved with the club, Kevin currently holds an ambassadorial role at the Stadium of Light.

'Every team needs someone who they can rely on during a match, someone who can make things happen if things are not going right, someone you would want next to you in the trenches, someone to do the hard work and show an example to the rest of the team, ...Kevin Ball is one of those players!

"A midfielder who always gave you one hundred per cent and led the team by example, he captained the team for Peter Reid when Sunderland had its best two finishes in the Premiership. A real legend on Wearside, Kevin has also been a coach and manager at the Stadium of Light, and is currently an ambassador for our club.'

Micky

JIM BAXTER

Arguably the finest midfielder ever produced from Scottish football, Jim Baxter first came to prominence with Rangers after starting his career at Raith Rovers. Nicknamed Slim Jim by the Ibrox supporters, his outstanding performances soon earned him international recognition. His one-man demolition of England at Wembley in 1962, when he scored both goals in Scotland's 2-1 victory over the Auld Enemy, guaranteed him a place in Scottish football folklore for all time.

A superb passer of the ball with a left foot often described as a magic wand, Jim was widely regarded as the finest left-sided midfielder in British football, and his standing on the world stage was recognised in 1963 when he was selected for the Rest of the World team to face England at Wembley in a special game arranged to celebrate 100 years of the Football Association.

The following year saw Jim's career come to a sudden halt when he suffered a broken leg in the closing stages of a European Cup-tie against Rapid Vienna in Austria, but when he recovered fitness the following year, his inevitable move south of the border arrived when he was signed by Sunderland for £72,500. An early sign of Jim's brilliance came in a game against Sheffield United early in his first season at Roker Park when he produced a virtuoso performance scoring two goals in an emphatic 4-1 victory.

On his day Jim Baxter had few equals, but he rarely reached those heights during his time at Roker Park. Nevertheless in 1967, he proved he was still capable of performing at the highest level when he produced another stunning display to help Scotland defeat reigning world champions England at Wembley. The sight of Slim Jim taunting the England players by playing keepie-uppie is still talked about to this day north of the border.

Another of Jim's truly great Sunderland performances came in a 1-0 victory over high-flying Nottingham Forest at Roker Park in November 1968, but it was a game that would signal the end of his career on Wearside. Forest boss Johnny Carey was so impressed by Slim Jim's performance that a few weeks later the Nottingham club tabled a bid of £100,000 for the mercurial Scot which was duly accepted by the Roker board. His time at Forest lasted less than eighteen months before Baxter was on his way back to Rangers on a free transfer.

Jim Baxter once said: 'I don't want to be a millionaire - I just want to live like one!' and that, in a nutshell, summed up Slim Jim's approach to life. He lived it to the full. Jim sadly passed away at the age of only 61.

"A proud Scotsman who came to Sunderland from Rangers towards the end of his career. Even so when you watched Slim, you could see he had qualities that no one else could dream of.

"Slim liked a little drink now and again, even coming in for training a little worse for wear, but you could still not get near him or take the ball away from him. Slim probably had the best left foot that any Sunderland supporter has ever seen."

18   Micky

GARY BENNETT

Born in Manchester, Gary began his professional career with Manchester City in 1979 where he played alongside his elder brother Dave. The pair then teamed up again at Cardiff City where the arrival of former Sunderland legend Len Ashurst as manager was about to shape Gary's future in the game. In the summer of 1984, Len moved back to his beloved Sunderland to take over the Roker Park hot-seat and immediately returned to his former club to clinch Gary's signature.

Playing in a midfield role, Gary's debut in red and white stripes could hardly have been more dramatic when he scored in the opening minutes of a 3-1 victory over Southampton. He then helped his new club reach the Milk Cup Final, only to lose to a solitary Norwich City goal. Worse was to follow however, as Sunderland's form dipped badly after the final, culminating in relegation to Division Two and the departure of manager Len Ashurst.

Sunderland then appointed Lawrie McMenemy as boss, a high profile figure who had earned a big reputation with his former club Southampton, but sadly failed miserably during his time on Wearside leaving the club on the brink of relegation to Division Three. However, one of the few successes from his time at Sunderland was the appointment of Gary Bennett as captain, who went on to lead the team to the Third Division Championship in 1988 and then promotion back to the top flight two years later. Now playing in the centre of Sunderland's defence, Gary was in the team that reached the FA Cup final in 1992. He went on to make almost 450 appearances during his eleven years at the club and his loyalty was rewarded with a testimonial against Rangers in July 1993. In November 1995, Gary joined Carlisle United and later played for Scarborough and Darlington where he had a brief spell as manager.

A great favourite with Sunderland fans, Gary still enjoys cult status on Wearside and is currently involved in coaching local youngsters. He is also a key figure with the 'Show Racism the Red Card' campaign, as well as commentating on Sunderland games on local radio.

"Another massive icon in Sunderland, Gary came to the club in July 1984 and was surprised to find that there was not many black people in the North East. He knew it would be hard for him, but to his credit he got stuck in, mixed with the community and became a popular member of our club.

"Gary came to us after spells at Manchester City and Cardiff, he went on to play 369 league games for us, 442 in all and was a very consistent centre-back. A very cool player who played similar to the modern day Rio Ferdinand, went on to play for Carlisle, Scarborough and Darlington. He made his home in Sunderland and is still with us where he is a big influence in the community."

Micky

JOE BOLTON

One of the hardest defenders ever to wear Sunderland's famous red and white striped shirt, Joe Bolton still remains a cult figure with those supporters who saw him play. Born in Birtley, Joe progressed through the ranks at Roker Park eventually making his first team debut in a Division Two fixture against Watford at Roker Park towards the end of the 1971/72 season.

The following season saw Sunderland's legendary FA Cup success, with Joe making his first appearance in the competition in both third round ties against Notts County. However, his progress was halted by the arrival of Ron Guthrie who held the number three shirt for the remainder of the competition and it was not until the promotion season of 1975/76 that Joe finally became established as the club's first choice left-back.

Joe's uncompromising style may have stretched the laws of the game on occasion, but he was a hugely popular player with the Roker fans who loved his never-say-die approach to the game. Few wingers got the better of Joe and the few that did were invariably left with the customary battle scars for their trouble. During his time at Sunderland Joe netted twelve goals although a penalty miss against Charlton Athletic on the final day of the 1977/78 season would have given him his first-ever hat-trick!

After helping Sunderland gain promotion in 1980, Joe finally severed his ties with the club to join Middlesbrough. A spell with Sheffield United followed and then a brief taste in management with Matlock Town, before he retired from the game and became a long-distance lorry driver.

"Joe was a class left-back who made 325 appearances in the red and white shirt, daft as a brush and hard as nails, but believe me, he was a top, top full-back. A skin head in his younger days, Joe was a right character, he became a cult figure at Sunderland with the crowd loving him for his no-nonsense way of playing - if a winger was threatening him he would simply take him out!

"I think the left-back position is, or has been, our strongest position over the years and Joe contributes greatly to that. Joe was my roommate when I was just starting in the first team and continued to be so until I left for Man City. We had some great trips away with the team and on holiday. The cup run was great for the two of us, both young lads enjoying life and we sat in the front of the bus, from our hotel to Wembley Stadium. Going up Wembley way that day and seeing all our supporters will be something both of us will never forget. Joe still lives local and while we don't see much of him these days, he will always be a true friend."

Micky

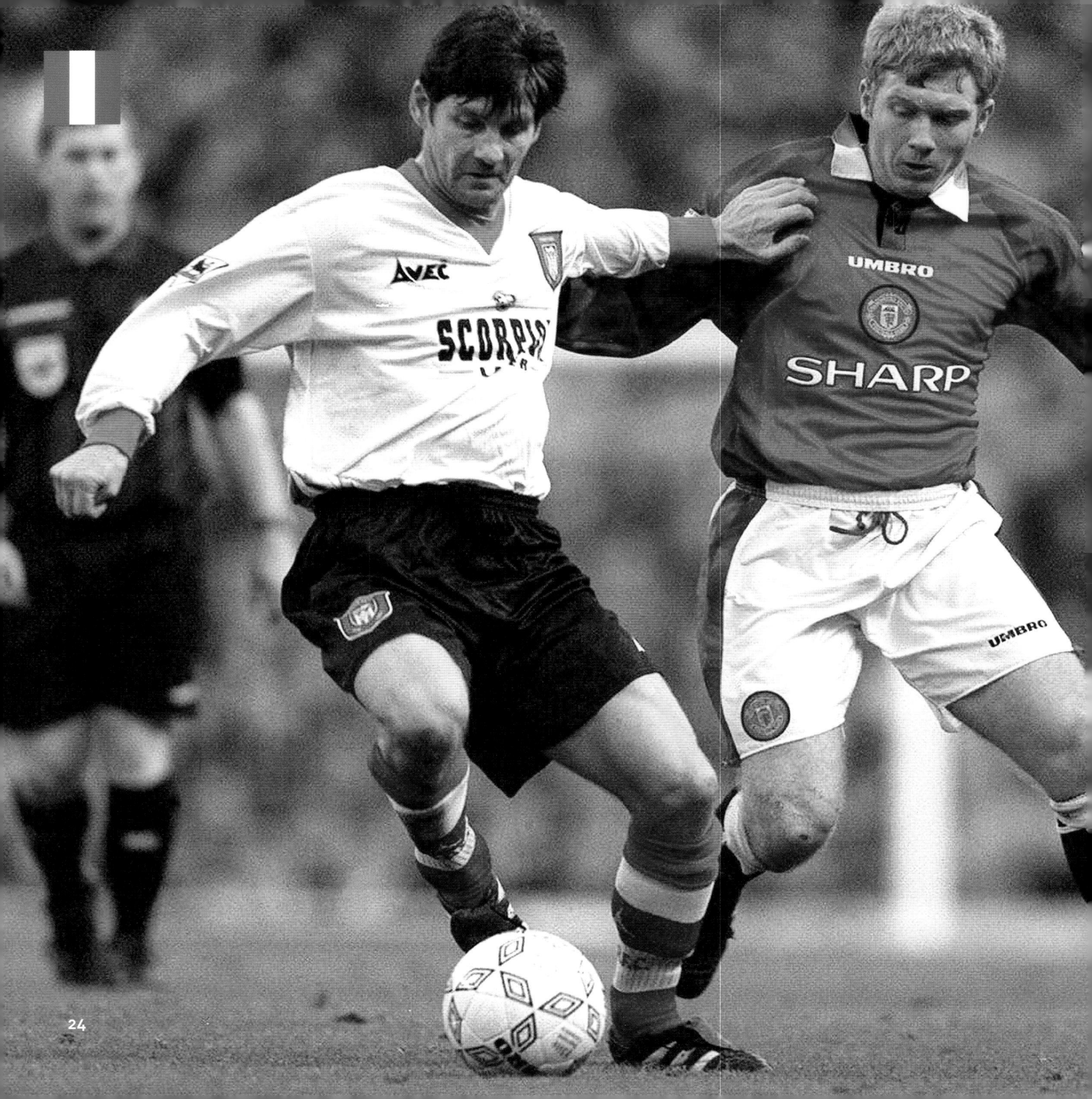
UMBRO
SHARP
UMBRO

PAUL BRACEWELL

Born on Merseyside, Paul Bracewell began his career as an apprentice with Stoke City in 1978, eventually signing professional forms two years later. After making his first team debut at Wolverhampton Wanderers just before his 18th birthday, Paul soon became established as a key performer in City's midfield where he was pretty much an ever-present for the best part of four seasons.

He joined Sunderland in July 1983, having been signed by his former Stoke City boss Alan Durban who had taken over the Roker Park hot-seat two years earlier. A great ball-winner in the midfield anchor-man role, Paul was hugely popular with the Roker faithful, but when Durban lost his job a year later, Paul was surprisingly sold to Everton by new manager Len Ashurst.

Paul's time at Goodison Park proved to be the most successful period of his playing career and he was a key performer in a great Everton side that went on to lift the League Championship and European Cup-Winners Cup. Already an Under-23 international he won three full caps for England during his time with the Toffees, before returning to Sunderland in September 1989.

Paul captained Sunderland in the 1992 FA Cup final against Liverpool, his fourth appearance in a final, all of which, sadly, ended in defeat. Soon afterwards, he somewhat surprisingly signed for arch-rivals Newcastle United, but three years later he returned to Roker Park for a third time in a player/assistant manager role at the start of the Peter Reid era that saw Sunderland win the First Division championship in 1996.

In 1996, Paul joined Fulham, where he took over as manager after Kevin Keegan left Craven Cottage to take over as England boss and he then had a brief spell in charge at Halifax Town. In 2013, Paul returned to Sunderland to take up a coaching role in the club's academy and is currently first-team coach working alongside new manager Sam Allardyce.

"A player with a great pedigree with almost 600 games in top flight football, 270 of them for Sunderland, Paul has had an amazing career.

"He was a tough central midfield player who never shirked a tackle which caused him to get lots of injuries, otherwise who knows how many league games he would have played!"

Micky

JODY CRADDOCK

Born in Redditch, Jody began his career at Cambridge United where he came under the influence of former Derby County and England centre-half Roy McFarland, who was manager at the Abbey Stadium at the time and a major influence on his development as a promising central defender.

Jody joined Sunderland in July 1997 with the £300,000 transfer taking place on the very day the Stadium of Light was officially opened and while he had been signed by manager Peter Reid as one for the future, his elevation to first-team football was rapid.

He made his debut a few months after signing, in a League Cup game against Bury and quickly formed a successful defensive partnership with Darren Williams. Unfortunately the season ended in major disappointment, when Sunderland lost on penalties to Charlton Athletic in the Division One Play-Off final at Wembley.

However, promotion was clinched in style the following year when they lifted the First Division title with a record 105 points, although Jody played only a handful of games after losing his place due to a calf injury. He regained his position in the side the following season and was an outstanding performer in the heart of Sunderland's defence as Peter Reid's team secured seventh place finishes in the Premier League in consecutive seasons.

After making well over 150 appearances for the club, Jody's career at the Stadium of Light came to a close during the 2003 close-season when he joined Wolverhampton Wanderers in a £1.75 million deal. He spent ten years with the Molineux club and his loyalty was rewarded with a testimonial game in which a Wolves XI beat a Sunderland XI 4-1 with Jody appearing for Wolves in the first half and Sunderland in the second.

"Jody was a solid and dependable centre-back and one of those thin wiry types who although not massive, would hit you with their knees, elbows, hips etc.

"He always gave one hundred per cent, which made him extremely popular with the fans. A lovely guy, Jody has taken up art since hanging up his boots and has sold a number of paintings."

Micky

JOHNNY CROSSAN

The early career of Irish international Johnny Crossan was certainly surrounded in controversy having been banned for life from British football after allegedly accepting illegal payments whilst playing for Derry City. Forced to play his football abroad, Johnny signed for Sparta Rotterdam yet amazingly continued to be selected for the Irish international team.

Johnny then moved on to join Standard Liege where he picked up a Belgian championship medal before his return to British shores was finally agreed in February 1962. Sunderland had shown a strong interest in Johnny since his Derry City days and the Wearside club played a major role in persuading the Irish League to lift the ban. Within days, the Irish international was unveiled at Roker Park following a £30,000 transfer and he marked his home debut by scoring twice in the 6-2 demolition of Grimsby Town.

In his second full season at Roker Park, Sunderland clinched promotion back to the top flight with Johnny finishing top scorer with 27 league and cup goals. A truly magnificent campaign should have been the springboard for even greater things but sadly, after the surprise departure of manager Alan Brown during the close-season, the team struggled in Division One. In mid-November, George Hardwick took over as manager and whilst he did steady the ship, his appointment signalled the end of Johnny's career at Roker Park and in February 1965 he was sold to Manchester City for £40,000. It was a decision that was greeted with a mixture of disbelief and anger by Sunderland fans, many of whom regarded the Irish international as the club's key player.

Sunderland's loss certainly proved to be very much City's gain and at Maine Road, Johnny was quickly installed as team captain, going on to lead City to the Second Division title in his first full season at the club. In 1967 he returned to the North East to join Middlesbrough and after spending three seasons at Ayresome Park he moved back to Belgium to join KSK Tongergen. Johnny finally hung up his boots in 1975 and headed home to Ireland where he later opened a sports shop in Londonderry.

"A true Irishman, Johnny was an inside-forward who was one of the best that came out of Ireland.

"He had a lazy looking approach to the game, but possessed fantastic ball control and was one of the best passers of the ball in the game. A team needs different types of players in the side to get the correct balance and Johnny was definitely the brains and quality of the 60s promotion team."

Micky

SHAUN ELLIOTT

Born in Haltwhistle, Northumberland, Shaun Elliott came through the ranks at Roker Park and broke into the first team during the 1976/77 season. He was handed his debut in an FA Cup third round tie at Wrexham with his first appearance in the league coming against Leicester City at Filbert Street a few days later. At the time, Sunderland were struggling desperately for survival in Division One and manager Jimmy Adamson, perhaps in desperation, decided to turn to youth in a bid to reverse the club's fortunes.

It was a decision that turned out to be a masterstroke as Shaun, along with other youngsters Gary Rowell and Kevin Arnott, took the league by storm. A game against Middlesbrough at Roker Park proved to be the turning point and having scored only once in their previous eleven league games, Sunderland netted four, followed by six in each of their next two games against West Bromwich Albion and West Ham United. Sadly, Sunderland's amazing revival fell just short and a 2-0 defeat at Everton in the final game of the season saw the club relegated back to Division Two after only one season in the top flight.

In those early days of his career, Shaun had operated in a midfield role, but eventually he was moved into the Roker back four, soon developing into an outstanding defender. In 1980 he was a key member of the Sunderland team that clinched promotion and also achieved international recognition when he won the first of his three England B caps.

The biggest disappointment in Shaun's Sunderland career came in 1985, when he captained the team in a great run in the Milk Cup, only to miss out on leading out his team at Wembley after being booked in the semi-final victory over Chelsea at Stamford Bridge. The following season, after 368 appearances for the club, his career at Roker Park came to an end when he was transferred to Norwich City. He then played for Blackpool and Colchester before a spell in American soccer brought his top-class playing career to a close.

"Shaun was a favourite with the fans because of his hundred per cent commitment in every game.

"He was a strong central-defender who loved a battle with centre-forwards, but he was also very good in the air, quick and a good passer of the ball."

Micky

31

MARCO GABBIADINI

One of the finest strikers in Sunderland's post-war history, Marco Gabbiadini exploded onto the scene when he arrived at Roker Park shortly after the start of the 1987/88 season. There were a few raised eyebrows when Sunderland manager Denis Smith returned to his former club York City to sign the young striker, but it was a decision that turned out to be a masterstroke.

Sunderland had slipped into English football's third tier for the first time ever and it was the arrival of Marco more than anything else that helped reverse the club's ailing fortunes. Quickly forming a brilliant striking partnership with the vastly experienced Eric Gates, Marco took the Third Division by storm, netting 21 goals to help Sunderland clinch the league title and promotion back to Division Two at the first time of asking. His pace, power and devastating finishing coupled with the subtle skills of Gates prompted the fans to nickname the pair, the G-Force.

Two years later, in 1990, promotion to Division One was achieved and the strength of the partnership was perhaps never better demonstrated than when they helped Sunderland to a memorable 2-0 victory over Newcastle United in the Division Two Play-Off semi-final second leg at St James' Park. After an early Gates' goal had given Sunderland the lead, the pair then combined brilliantly in the closing stages for Marco to surge into the box and drive home the vital second goal. To cap a great season, Marco picked up two Under-23 caps for England and was then selected for the B international against Czechoslovakia at Roker Park.

Sadly, Sunderland's stay in the top flight lasted only one season and soon afterwards the club took the decision to cash in on their prized asset. In October 1991, only a week after netting a breath-taking six-minute hat-trick against Charlton Athletic, Marco was sold to Crystal Palace for a fee reported to be in the region of £1.8 million. However, his stay at Selhurst Park lasted only a matter of months and he moved on to Derby County where he enjoyed five successful seasons with the Rams.

After loan spells with Birmingham City and Oxford United, Marco joined Stoke City before heading back to the North East to join Darlington. Finally, after three successful seasons with Northampton where he continued to score regularly, he finished his playing career with Hartlepool, where injury forced him to retire from the game in January 2004. Marco now runs an award-winning hotel in York and is also a football pundit on local radio.

"Another one of our better purchases, Marco signed for us from York City and very soon became a great favourite with the crowd because of his all-action, direct play.

"He was a striker who loved to charge through the middle of defences using his strength and pace."
Micky

ERIC GATES

A hugely talented forward who could operate either in a midfield or striking role, Ferryhill-born Eric Gates began his career at Ipswich Town as a youngster and was a member of the club's highly-talented youth team that lifted the FA Youth Cup in 1973. After signing a professional contract, Eric went on to enjoy almost 13 seasons with Ipswich during the highly successful Bobby Robson era and during his time at Portman Road he won two full international caps when he played for England in the World Cup qualifying games against Norway and Romania in 1981.

One of Lawrie McMenemy's first signings, Eric joined Sunderland during the 1985 close-season, but it was following the arrival of Marco Gabbiadini two years later that his career at Roker Park really began to blossom. Known as the G-Force, with Eric's subtle skills and Marco's lightning pace, the pair quickly developed a devastating strike partnership and shared 40 goals during Sunderland's 1988 Third Division Championship season, with Eric netting four in the 7-0 victory over Southend United.

Arguably the most memorable game for the G-Force came in the 1990 Second Division Play-Off semi-final second leg against Newcastle United at St James' Park, when Eric opened the scoring and then released Marco to seal the tie and take Sunderland to Wembley.

Eric spent five years at Roker Park making over 200 appearances and netting 54 goals before joining Carlisle United. He later had a spell commentating on Sunderland games and also teamed up with Malcolm Macdonald and Bernie Slaven on local radio's, Three Legends programme.

"A player who was very popular with the supporters, Eric teamed up with Marco to form a very powerful and dangerous partnership upfront where Marco had the pace and power and Eric had the guile and skill to open up defences.

"An exceptionally talented player, he could make chances for other people as well as being a good goal-scorer in his own right. Still living in the area, Eric went on to have a very successful career on local radio and is often at Sunderland games at the Stadium of Light."

Micky

MICHAEL GRAY

One of a select band of Sunderland-born players to represent England at full international level, Michael Gray was an outstanding left-back who gave Sunderland great service and enjoyed a lengthy career in the top-class game.

Born in Castletown on the outskirts of the city, Michael could hardly have made a more explosive start to his Sunderland career, when he scored with a terrific shot from outside the box, in the first minute of his debut against Barnsley at Roker Park in December 1992.

Michael went on to play for five managers during his SAFC career, although his best period was undoubtedly the Peter Reid era when he enjoyed two promotions to the Premier League, in 1996 and 1999, and picked up three full international caps for England. He is also in the record books, being the first player to score for Sunderland in the Premier League, a seventh-minute strike in a 4-1 victory over Nottingham Forest at the City Ground on 21 August 1996.

Undoubtedly the worst moment in his career came in 1998 when he missed the vital spot-kick in the 1999 Division One Play-Off final penalty shoot-out against Charlton Athletic at Wembley. However, he bounced back in typical fashion and after helping Sunderland clinch the championship the following season, became one of the star players in the team that claimed two seventh place finishes in the Premiership in 2000 and 2001.

After making over 400 appearances for the club and netting 17 goals, Michael's Sunderland career finally came to a close in January 2004, when after a four-month loan spell at Celtic, he joined Blackburn Rovers on a free transfer. He later played for Leeds United, Wolverhampton Wanderers and Sheffield Wednesday before retiring from the game at the end of the 2009/10 season to take up a career in media work.

"A left-back that could play in any era, Michael liked nothing better than sprinting up that left touch line and getting really telling crosses in for his forwards.

"At Sunderland he formed a superb left-sided partnership with Allan Johnston and at his peak he was one of the best left-backs in the English game, deservedly winning three full international caps for England, who at the time were managed by Kevin Keegan."
Micky

RON GUTHRIE

Signed from Newcastle United by Bob Stokoe in January 1973, Ron Guthrie added some much-needed experience to the left side of Sunderland's defence. A solidly-built left-back, he had become something of a fringe player at St James' Park, yet within a few short months of joining SAFC he was picking up a FA Cup-winners medal at Wembley.

A consistent and defensively sound performer, few opponents caused problems for Ron and during the FA Cup run he nullified the threat of some top wing-men of the day, including the likes of Mike Summerbee of Manchester City and Leeds United's Peter Lorimer. Although never noted for his goal-scoring, he weighed in with a vital goal in the sixth round tie against Luton Town at Roker Park, a volley on the turn executed with some style to secure Sunderland's place in the semi-final.

In the two seasons that followed the FA Cup triumph, Sunderland came close to clinching promotion back to the top flight, but when they finally made it at the third attempt in 1976, Ron had moved on, having lost his place to the up-and-coming Joe Bolton. He joined non-league Blyth Spartans and was a key member of the team that reached the FA Cup fifth round in 1978, losing narrowly to Wrexham in a replay in front of over 42,000 at St James' Park.

After retiring from the game Ron was a milkman and later worked as a delivery driver for a Newcastle department store.

"Ron was a strong no-nonsense player who got on with his job very quietly.

"Although he was a former Newcastle United player and had supported the Magpies all his life, when he came to Sunderland he gave us everything he had. Although not the quickest, Ron was so strong and brave, not many wingers got the better of him."

Micky

VIC HALOM

When Vic Halom signed for Sunderland in February 1973, he might have been something of an unknown quantity to Sunderland fans, but Roker boss Bob Stokoe knew exactly the type of player he was signing, having managed Halom some years earlier at Charlton Athletic.

A centre-forward in the traditional mould, yet remarkably skilful for a big man, Vic became an instant hit with Sunderland fans when he netted a stunning goal in the fifth round replay against Manchester City soon after his arrival at Roker Park. In the game, later voted Roker's greatest ever match, his strike followed a slick Sunderland passing move and when he received the ball on the right corner of the Fulwell End penalty area. He unleashed a right-foot shot of such power that City 'keeper Joe Corrigan could only look on as a helpless spectator as the ball rocketed into the top corner of the net.

Vic was on target again in the semi-final against Arsenal at Hillsborough when he produced arguably his best-ever performance in a Sunderland shirt, particularly in the first half when he ran the Gunners defence ragged. That said, his hat-trick against Derby County in the League Cup the following season would certainly take some beating.

On the Roker terraces, Vic became something of a cult figure, a swashbuckling centre-forward who always played the game with a smile on his face. He remained on Wearside for over three years, picking up a championship medal when Sunderland clinched the Second Division title in 1976, before joining Oldham Athletic soon afterwards.

After injury brought his playing career to a close in 1981, Vic tried his hand in football management, first with Barrow followed by spells with Rochdale, Burton Albion and then back in the North East with North Shields. After retiring from the game he worked in the water industry and stood for the Liberal Democrats in Sunderland North in the 1992 General Election before moving abroad to live in Bulgaria.

"A smashing fella and a real character, Vic led our team from the front with a passion not seen nowadays.

"He was brave and strong, the perfect target man who loved to mix it with big centre-backs and more often than not he came out on top. Vic now lives abroad, but still comes to see us a few times a year, something we all look forward to as he is great company."

Micky

GORDON HARRIS

Another product of the great Burnley youth system of the late 1950s, Gordon was initially employed as a left-winger before moving to a more central midfield role. A tough, uncompromising character, few opponents took liberties with Gordon who had a reputation as one of the hardest players in the game, although at his peak, he was also regarded as one of the most skilful midfielders around.

Gordon was in the Burnley team that lifted the League Championship in 1960 and played in the FA Cup final at Wembley two years later when they lost 3-1 to Tottenham Hotspur. In 1966, having previously been capped at Under-23 level, he won full international honours when he was picked to play for England against Poland at Goodison Park.

Gordon was signed by Sunderland in 1968 and whilst he may have been coming towards the end of his top-class career, he was still able to demonstrate those qualities that had established him as an international-class player. Most of all however, it was his ability to read the game and orchestrate proceedings from the middle of the park that caught the eye and whilst Sunderland were relegated at the end of his second full season at the club, he was without doubt one of the better players during a hugely disappointing campaign.

Gordon stayed at Roker Park for four seasons before moving into non-league football with South Shields. He later worked in the coal industry and died in 2014, aged 73.

"Another player I used to watch while I was an apprentice, Gordon was very laid back and nothing seemed to bother him. I remember him as a very strong midfielder and someone you would not want to mess with.

"Gordon joined Sunderland from Burnley in 1967 playing 135 games for us and scoring 16 goals.
He was nicknamed 'the General' as he was a born leader and always led from the front.
Gordon would always be where the action was and was certainly a player you would always want in your team."

Micky

MARTIN HARVEY

Born in Belfast, Martin Harvey was signed by Sunderland manager Alan Brown in September 1958, having been rejected by Burnley following trials at Turf Moor. Martin's elevation to first-team football was rapid and he was handed his debut against Plymouth Argyle a little over a year after arriving at Roker Park. However, it would be another five years before he would finally become an established regular in the team.

Throughout that period, he acted as understudy to Sunderland's legendary wing-half Stan Anderson and whilst he was capped at full international level by Northern Ireland, it was not until the Sunderland skipper was sold to Newcastle United in October 1963 that Martin finally made the number four shirt his own. Ironically, it was that same month that Martin took over from another footballing legend, Danny Blanchflower, in the Northern Ireland team.

The 1963/64 season was an outstanding one for Martin as Sunderland won promotion back to Division One with the newly formed half-back line of Harvey, Hurley and McNab proving to be the backbone of a fine side that is still talked about to this day. Although the team generally struggled in the top flight, Martin remained a consistent performer, and his forceful running, ability in the tackle and constructive play made him a great favourite with Sunderland fans.

Martin was eventually handed the captaincy by Sunderland boss Alan Brown, but sadly, his career came to a sudden end when he picked up an injury at Norwich in 1972 and was forced to quit the game at the age of 31. He had made over 350 senior appearances for Sunderland and was awarded a testimonial against Newcastle United in recognition of his services to the club.

A brief spell at Carlisle United was Martin's only taste of football management and thereafter he held coaching roles at a variety of clubs including Plymouth Argyle, Raith Rovers and Millwall.

"Martin was my favourite player when I first started to go and watch Sunderland in the late sixties.

"As a youngster it was Martin Harvey who I wanted to be. Big and strong, I loved the way he used to tackle, sliding in from the side, usually with his left foot which made me want to use my left foot and that helped me later in my career. After I joined Sunderland as an apprentice, I used to babysit for Martin and his wife."

Micky

45

GEORGE HERD

A star performer in the great Sunderland side of the 60s, George was the engine-room in the Roker midfield for virtually the entire decade. A skilful and creative player, he had already been capped by Scotland at full international level when he arrived from Clyde, following a £42,000 transfer just before the end of the 1960/61 season.

Signed by manager Alan Brown, George proved to be major coup for the club having almost joined arch-rivals Newcastle United only for Sunderland to arrive on the scene at the eleventh hour and clinch the deal. In his first two seasons on Wearside, Sunderland came within a whisker of clinching promotion, but it was third time lucky in 1964 when they finished as runners-up to Leeds United.

Although he was very much the creative player in the side, George netted 13 goals in a season that also saw a great run in the FA Cup. Older fans may well recall George, a fitness fanatic, treating the Roker fans to an impromptu display of acrobatics as the team paraded around the pitch celebrating the 2-1 victory over Charlton Athletic which clinched the club's return to Division One.

In the seasons that followed, Sunderland generally struggled in the top flight and George was a key figure in ensuring their survival before they were finally relegated at the end of the 1969/70 season. Soon afterwards, after making well over 300 appearances and netting 55 goals for the club, George called time on his Roker Park career and moved down the coast to join Hartlepool. After retirement he held various coaching appointments with the North East's big three and also enjoyed two spells in Kuwait.

"George was another Scotsman who played wide on the right side of midfield, a busy little player who always gave his all for the team. Although George was only small in stature, he had a big heart and feared no-one as well as being the fittest guy I have ever come across.

"In training he would do somersaults, forward rolls and jump over other players - great to watch! After his playing days were over George became a coach at Sunderland, looking after the youth team and when I started my apprenticeship he was one of my coaches, which was good for me as he was a stickler for discipline, which was certainly what I needed at the time!"

Micky

BILLY HUGHES

One of the most exciting forwards to come through the Roker Park ranks during the 1960s, Billy made his first-team debut against Liverpool, shortly after his eighteenth birthday, in a Sunderland team that included no fewer than seven Scots. Spotted by Sunderland scout Tom Rutherford, Billy almost joined Celtic, where his elder brother John had become one of the key members of a team that would soon become the first British side to lift the European Cup. Fortunately for Sunderland, Billy chose a career south of the border where he soon became established as a first-team regular and a great favourite with the Roker faithful.

The 1973 FA Cup run was undoubtedly the highlight of Billy's career and his performance in the fifth round replay against Manchester City at Roker Park when he netted two goals in a magnificent 3-1 victory demonstrated that, at his peak, there were few better strikers in the English game. It was during the 1973 campaign that Billy's brother John, joined the Roker Park ranks following a move from Crystal Palace, although the mouth-watering prospect of the Hughes brothers leading the Sunderland attack never materialised, when an injury sustained during his debut against Millwall effectively ended John's career.

There were many outstanding moments during Billy's Sunderland career, not least his two goals against Manchester United at Old Trafford in 1974 which silenced the 60,000 home fans and international recognition finally arrived the following year, when he won his only full international cap for Scotland in the 1-1 draw against Sweden. Success continued in 1975/76 when he helped Sunderland clinch the Second Division title, but a year later he was allowed to leave the club to join Derby County in a £30,000 transfer.

However, his stay at the Baseball Ground lasted only a matter of months when, following the arrival of new boss Tommy Docherty, he was somewhat surprisingly transferred to neighbours Leicester City. A move to Carlisle United followed and then a brief spell in California with San Jose Earthquakes before he retired from the game in 1980.

"The life and soul of the party, Billy was my best friend at the time and he and his wife Linda took me under their wing and looked after me. Billy was our most under-rated player and had everything a striker needed.

"He was very quick, skilful and brave with a little cockiness and he could score goals. He should have gone on to be a top First Division player but Billy being Billy, he was happy with what he had. He loved a cigarette before a game but it never stopped him tormenting defences every week."

Micky

CHARLIE HURLEY

Known to the fans as the King, Charlie Hurley remains the most popular player in Sunderland's long and illustrious history, a fact which was endorsed in 1979 when supporters voted him their Player of the Century, at the club's centenary dinner - not bad for a man who did not want to join the club in the first place!

In fact, back in 1957, it took all the persuasive powers of Sunderland manager Alan Brown to convince the young Millwall and Republic of Ireland centre-half that his footballing future lay at Roker Park. Brown promised Charlie that he planned to build a new team around him and whilst it probably seemed a bit far-fetched to the youngster at the time, that's exactly what the Roker boss did.

Charlie's first few performances in a Sunderland shirt could hardly have been described as inspirational, as the Roker defence leaked no fewer than 13 goals in his first two games and when the club were relegated from Division One for the first time ever at the end of the season, the future certainly looked bleak. However, within a few short years Charlie had developed into arguably the finest centre-half in British football and in 1964 he led the team to promotion, just as Brown had predicted. To cap a marvellous year, he also finished as runner-up to England and West Ham captain Bobby Moore in the Footballer of the Year awards.

Charlie was also one of the first defenders to venture up the field for corners and free-kicks, an innovative tactic at the time and a one that worked to devastating effect creating havoc in the opposition penalty area as he set up chances for his teammates as well as scoring a few himself. The fans loved it and throughout the 60s the chant of 'Charlie, Charlie...' would echo around Roker Park every time the home side won a corner.

On the international front, Charlie was a stalwart performer for the Republic of Ireland and after winning his first cap in a World Cup qualifier against England at Dalymount Park at the age of only 20 in 1957, he went on to appear a further 39 times for his country. His Roker Park career spanned almost twelve years during which he made 400 appearances and netted 26 goals before joining Bolton Wanderers during the 1969 close-season.

Charlie then had a spell in management with Reading and he received a tremendous reception from Sunderland supporters when he brought his team to Roker Park for a fourth round FA Cup-tie in 1973. After retiring from the game in 1977, Charlie enjoyed a lengthy career in sales and now lives in quiet retirement in Hoddesdon in Hertfordshire.

"King Charlie, captain of the promotion-winning side of the sixties, was a fantastic man who always had time for everyone at the club, whether you were the cleaner, groundsman or apprentice, as I was. Charlie was voted Player of the Century not just because of his exceptional football ability, but also for the way he represented the club in every aspect - a great man in every sense!

"I remember the first day I moved to Manchester City, who at the time were captained by Mike Summerbee. From the moment I walked into the dressing room, all Mike wanted to tell me about was the day he beat Charlie Hurley in the air in front of the Roker End!"

Micky

CECIL IRWIN

Born in Ellington, Northumberland, Cecil was chased by a number of top clubs after appearing for Northumberland Schools as a youngster and had trials with Burnley before being approached by Sunderland. The decision to join the club he had supported as a boy from the terraces was an easy one and he signed amateur forms at Roker Park during the summer of 1958.

At the time, Sunderland manager Alan Brown had begun a rebuilding programme, built very much around young players and Cecil's elevation to first-team football came only a few months after joining the club. He made his first-team debut in September 1958 in a Division Two game against Ipswich Town at Roker Park at the age of only 16 years and 165 days, replacing Sunderland's regular right-back Jack Hedley.

Ironically, in the left-back position that day, was a young Len Ashurst, who was also making his first appearance at senior level and in the years ahead the two youngsters would become established as Sunderland's first choice full-back pairing.

Cecil won eight Youth international caps for England during this period and whilst he continued to appear regularly for Sunderland, it was the 1963/64 season before he finally became established as the club's first choice right-back. It was also the season that saw Sunderland clinch promotion back to the top flight in a truly memorable campaign that included a great run in the FA Cup when they beat League champions Everton, before bowing out of the competition after three epic encounters with Manchester United.

Tall, powerfully built and hard in the tackle, Cecil was a great favourite with the Roker Park fans who loved his ventures up the right flank and his pin-point crosses for the likes of Nick Sharkey and Neil Martin. Cecil played over 350 games for Sunderland in a career spanning 14 years, his only goal coming from long-range effort in a 3-1 victory over Nottingham Forest in October 1968.

Cecil severed his ties with Sunderland in the summer of 1972 and took over as manager of Southern League club Yeovil Town. Three years later, he retired from the game and returned to the North East where he ran a newsagents in Ashington for many years.

"Part of the great sixties' side, a right-back very similar to Dick Malone. Cecil was a good defender who loved to go forward, a proper overlapping full-back. Cecil also helped me get noticed by Sunderland's scouts - thank you Cecil!"

Micky

53

KENWYNE JONES

Born in Trinidad and Tobago, Kenwyne Jones began his career in British football with Southampton, soon becoming one of the most sought-after strikers outside the Premier League. Eventually it was newly-promoted Sunderland that clinched Kenwyne's signature just after the start of the 2007/08 season, with Stern John heading in the opposite direction in a deal valued at around £6 million.

Kenwyne netted his first goal for his new club in a 2-1 victory over Reading at the Stadium of Light and was soon attracting the attention of a number of top Premier League clubs, with Liverpool reportedly being prepared to offer Peter Crouch in an exchange deal. After Sunderland manager Roy Keane publically stated that Jones was going nowhere, Kenwyne continued to produce some brilliant performances with his acrobatic goal-scoring celebrations becoming the trademark of his game and after his first season at the club many were comparing him to Chelsea's legendary striker Didier Drogba.

However, Kenwyne's progress was halted during the 2008 close-season when he suffered knee ligament damage in a collision with England goalkeeper David James while playing for Trinidad and Tobago. It was some months before he returned to first-team action for Sunderland, coming on as a second-half substitute in a memorable 2-1 victory over arch-rivals Newcastle United at the Stadium of Light. Soon afterwards, Kenwyne signed a four-and-a-half-year contract, but the following year, after making over 100 appearances and netting 28 goals, he decided to sever his ties with the club and join Stoke City in a club-record deal of £8 million.

Kenwyne then enjoyed a spell with Cardiff City before joining Bournemouth on loan in March 2015, helping them clinch the Championship title and promotion to the Premier League.

"I can see a lot of raised eyebrows at seeing Kenwyne Jones in my top fifty and I can understand why, but Kenwyne was a player I really loved to watch, a centre-forward who really could have been as good as Drogba of Chelsea.

"He had everything that a top athlete or footballer would want - over six feet tall, excellent physique, strength and above all else, so very quick. His celebration after scoring was also something special to see and Kenwyne was a great a favourite with Sunderland fans during his time at the club."

Micky

BOBBY KERR

Born in Alexandria, Dunbartonshire, Bobby Kerr was spotted by Sunderland chief scout Charlie Ferguson and arrived at Roker Park during the 1963 close-season. Although small in stature, Bobby made a huge impact when he made his first-team debut four years later by scoring the only goal of the game against Manchester City in the dying minutes.

He would soon prove that this was no 'flash in the pan' by netting a further six goals in the next ten games. However, his baptism in English football was brought to a shuddering halt when he sustained a broken leg in a collision with Norman Hunter in a fifth round FA Cup tie at Roker Park. It would be 18 months before he returned to first-team action, but in the years that followed Bobby soon became established in the Sunderland first team, eventually taking over the captain's arm-band from Martin Harvey.

He will, of course, be best remembered for lifting the FA Cup in 1973 when Sunderland manager Bob Stokoe dubbed him 'The Little General' in recognition of his leadership qualities and tactical know-how. Bobby played in every game in the cup run and for the best part of ten seasons he was almost a permanent fixture in the Sunderland team. In the campaigns between 1971/72 and 1975/76, he never made less than 40 appearances and picked up a Second Division championship medal in 1976 when Sunderland finally made it back to English football's top flight.

Bobby's Roker Park career eventually came to an end in March 1979 when he teamed up with his old Sunderland boss Bob Stokoe at Blackpool, but a serious hip injury sustained in a game against Bury limited his progress at Bloomfield Road. After only 22 appearances for the Tangerines, he returned to the North East to join Hartlepool, before retiring from the game at the end of the 1981/82 season.

After football, Bobby went into the pub trade and still lives on Wearside where he remains a legend - the only man alive to have lifted a major trophy for Sunderland!

"The smallest captain to lift the FA Cup, but what he lacked in height he made up for in heart. Bobby was the perfect captain at the time, always kept himself to himself and let you know what he wanted from you on the pitch.

"Not the most skilful midfielder but as I've said, he had the biggest heart and always gave one hundred per cent. He has become a close friend and I love his company - a very funny guy who is loved by all Sunderland supporters."

Micky

57

SEBASTIAN LARSSON

Seb's career in the English game began with Arsenal, but it was with Birmingham City where he first came to prominence, earning a reputation as an outstanding right-sided midfielder and something of a set-play specialist. At St Andrew's, he played under manager Steve Bruce and when the City boss took over at the Stadium of Light, Seb became one of his most astute signings when he joined Sunderland on a free transfer under the Bosman Ruling during the 2011 close-season.

An established Swedish international, Seb marked his debut for his new club with a stunning volley to earn a 1-1 draw against Liverpool on the opening day of the 2011/12 season and when he netted a brilliant free-kick against Arsenal at the Emirates soon afterwards, Arsene Wenger commented that his former player was 'probably the best free-kick taker in the Premier League'.

Arguably the most memorable goal so far in Seb's Sunderland career came in Martin O'Neill's first match as manager, a stunning strike two minutes into stoppage time that sealed a 2-1 victory over Blackburn Rovers and helped ease the club's relegation worries. He also netted the only goal of the game against Manchester United during Sunderland's 'Great Escape' at the end of the 2013/14 season.

Seb has proved to be one of Sunderland's most popular players during recent times and his whole-hearted performances for the team were recognised in 2015, when supporters voted him their Player of the Year.

"Seb is the only player currently playing for Sunderland who made it into my fifty, because quite simply, he always gives everything he has every time he pulls on the famous red and white stripes.

"His work-rate and commitment are fantastic. Having had the pleasure of meeting Seb a few times, I can tell you he is also one of the nicest guys you could ever wish to meet."

Micky

DICK
MALONE

Born in Motherwell, Dick began his professional career with Ayr United, where he soon gained a reputation as a powerful attacking full-back with an eye for goal. International recognition followed when he was selected for Scotland's Under-23 match against France at Hampden Park in December 1969 and soon afterwards he was attracting the attention of a number of clubs south of the border. Leeds United and Fulham were keen to sign the Scot, but it was Sunderland manager Alan Brown who convinced Dick that his footballing future lay on Wearside.

However, it was under new manager Bob Stokoe that Dick's career at Roker Park really began to flourish, particularly during the 1973 FA Cup run and his performance in the final to nullify the threat of Eddie Gray was a major factor in helping Sunderland lift the trophy.

Although a regular goal-scorer in Scotland, Dick managed to find the net just twice during his seven years at the club, but both were real collector's items. The first was a forty-yard rocket and the second a brilliant solo effort, when he took on the Portsmouth defence before rounding the 'keeper to slot the ball into the empty net!

After picking up a Second Division championship medal in 1976, Dick spent another season at Roker Park before moving down the road to join Hartlepool United. A year later, he was on the move again, this time to Blackpool where he teamed up with his former Sunderland boss Bob Stokoe. After two years at Bloomfield Road Dick headed back to Scotland to play for Queen of the South, before retiring from the game at the end of the 1981/82 season.

"Before the Cup Final, Bob Stokoe was worried about how Dick would cope with Eddie Gray, the brilliant Leeds United left-winger.

"Everyone in the media was predicting Gray would be the match-winner, with people like Jackie Charlton predicting that Dick would be our weak link in the final. How wrong they all were, the Scotsman had a fantastic game defensively, so much so that Gray was taken off in the second half!"

Micky

NEIL MARTIN

Neil Martin was already established as a prolific goalscorer north of the border when Sunderland paid out a club record fee of £50,000 to secure the services of Hibernian's Tranent-born centre-forward in October 1965.

Neil had netted over 100 goals in Scottish football and he continued in the same vein as he settled into a Sunderland side that also included another recently-signed Scottish star, Jim Baxter. A centre-forward in the traditional mould, Neil was particularly good in the air, but with no small degree of skill and he quickly became a great favourite with the Roker fans.

His first season on Wearside was hampered by injury, but in the 1966/67 campaign, the big striker was a revelation, hitting 26 goals to become the club's leading scorer, his exceptional ability in the air and powerful shooting making him one of Division One's top strikers.

Neil was capped three times for Scotland during his time with Sunderland and was leading the goal-scoring charts again in February 1968 when he was surprisingly sold to Coventry City for £90,000, on the same day that manager Ian McColl was sacked. He continued to find the target with his new club and later with Nottingham Forest, eventually equalling his record of north of the border, by scoring over 100 goals in the top-class game. Now retired, Neil lives back in his home town of Tranent, near Edinburgh.

"Neil was a big, strong, hard-hitting target-man, who was great at running the channels and holding the ball up for the rest of his teammates to get near him and join in.

"Probably his main asset was his heading ability, you always knew that if you crossed the ball into the box the defenders and goalkeeper would be troubled by the brave Neil Martin."

Micky

JIMMY McNAB

A Scotland Schoolboy international, Jimmy McNab was a stalwart performer for Sunderland throughout the 1960s. A terrific servant for the club, Jimmy made well over 300 appearances in a Roker Park career spanning over ten years. He made his debut in a Division Two game against Ipswich Town alongside two other debutants who would go on to become legendary figures at the club, Cecil Irwin and Len Ashurst. He held his position in the side for the next nine games before tragedy struck when he sustained a broken leg in a game at Rotherham.

Fully recovered, he returned to the side less than a year later and thereafter was pretty much an ever-present in a Sunderland team chasing promotion back to Division One. Promotion was finally achieved in 1964 with the half-back line of Harvey, Hurley and McNab firmly established as the backbone of the side and also widely regarded as the finest in the club's history.

A consistent performer who was noted for his tough-tackling and uncompromising approach to the game, Jimmy played 37 games during the promotion campaign. He missed only five games in the run-in, following an injury sustained in the 0-0 draw against Norwich City.

He briefly lost his coveted number 6 shirt, after the arrival of Jim Baxter in 1965, but continued to perform for the team in a more forward role and occasionally at left-back. Jimmy's final Sunderland appearance came in a 1-1 draw at Blackpool in January 1967 and soon afterwards he joined Preston North End where he gave great service during his seven-year stay at Deepdale. Jimmy then moved on to Stockport County before retiring from the game in 1976 to take up a career in insurance. His services to Sunderland Football Club were finally rewarded with a testimonial match in May 1999 at the Stadium of Light where he came off the bench to slot home a perfectly executed penalty. Sadly, in June 2006, Jimmy died at the age of 66 following a short illness.

"Sadly no longer with us, Jim was the final part of the famous Harvey-Hurley-McNab trio, surely one of Sunderland's best-ever half-back lines. Jimmy was a player known for his no-nonsense attitude who took no prisoners, a very hard Scotsman with a great left foot that could kill anyone."

Micky

65

JIMMY MONTGOMERY

Quite simply, one of Sunderland's greatest-ever players who remains a legend at the club to this day. Born and brought up on Wearside, his first-team debut came in a League Cup tie against Walsall at Roker Park in October 1961 and after that, he was pretty much a permanent fixture in the team captained by the great Charlie Hurley that many regard a Sunderland's finest post-war side. Promotion to Division One was gained in the 1963/64 season, an outstanding campaign that also saw epic FA Cup games against League champions Everton and Manchester United.

Whilst Sunderland struggled in the top flight, Monty remained in outstanding form and having been capped by England at Under-23 level, it seemed only a matter of time before full international honours would follow. Many felt he was the favourite to be selected as number two to Gordon Banks for the 1970 World Cup, but when he was overlooked, it became apparent that he would never receive that elusive first cap.

The 1973 FA Cup final against Leeds United was, of course, the highlight of Monty's career and his incredible double save to deny Leeds United's Peter Lorimer has, quite rightly, been voted Wembley's Greatest-Ever Save. Yet those who played alongside him or watched him from the terraces, would no doubt be able to recall countless saves of equal quality produced during a truly outstanding career at the club.

After helping Sunderland to the Division Two title in 1976, he was somewhat surprisingly sold to Birmingham City a few months later. There then followed spells at Southampton and Nottingham Forest, where he picked up a European Cup winners medal after being on the bench for the 1980 final against Hamburg.

Nowadays, Monty is Global Ambassador at Sunderland Football Club and in June 2015 he was awarded the British Empire Medal in the Queen's birthday honours in recognition of his services to football, a fitting tribute for a true Wearside legend.

"Monty has been a great servant to Sunderland, as a player, coach and now in his new role as the club's Global Ambassador. As a goalkeeper, he will always be remembered for his great double save in the cup final, first pushing away Trevor Cherrie's header (which I always tell him he should have caught) then his one-handed save off Peter Lorimer, which really was something special.

"However, having played with Monty on so many occasions, I have seen him make numerous great saves, some even better than that one, although the cup final save is, of course, his most important. He was desperately unlucky to play in an era that had so many great 'keepers, otherwise he would surely have received full international honours."
Micky

GEORGE MULHALL

Born in Falkirk the son of a miner, George Mulhall was one of three brothers, all of whom had a gift for the game and made the grade in league football north of the border. George however, was far and away the most talented and after making his name with Aberdeen and being capped by Scotland against Northern Ireland at full international level, he was signed by Sunderland early in the 1962/63 season.

A tough left-winger with pace and the ability to deliver pin-point crosses, George made his debut in red and white stripes in an away game at Rotherham in September 1962 and when Sunderland clinched promotion almost two years later he had not missed a single league game. George held the number eleven shirt throughout the 1960s, his skilful wing play and goal-scoring exploits making him a hugely popular figure with Sunderland fans.

He picked up a further two caps for Scotland during his time at Roker Park, both also against Northern Ireland, before going on to make 289 appearances for Sunderland, netting an impressive 67 goals. In 1969, George moved to South Africa to join Cape Town City where he went on to help them lift the League and Cup.

After returning to England in 1971, he joined Halifax Town in a coaching capacity before eventually being promoted to manager. George then enjoyed spells in charge at Bradford City and Bolton before returning to Halifax Town, where he was rewarded with a testimonial match against Sunderland in 1998.

"A left-winger that would be worth millions if he was playing today. George was not a big guy, but when you got the ball out to him on that left wing, you knew he would take the full-back on and try to get a cross in and more often than not, he did just that.

"George also had a reputation for having one of the hardest shots in the English game at the time and scored a fair number of goals during his Sunderland career."

Micky

RICHARD ORD

A Sunderland fan as a youngster, Dickie Ord fulfilled a lifetime dream when he made his debut in November 1987, and his introduction to first-team football could hardly have been more memorable as a rampant Sunderland side put seven goals past Southend United!

Dickie made only a handful of outings during the season that saw Sunderland lift the Third Division title, but the following campaign he made 31 league appearances for the side. A powerful central defender, Dickie was equally at home playing at left-back, but it was in the centre of Sunderland's defence where he eventually became established as a first-team regular and in 1991 he was capped by England at Under-21 level.

In the 1995/96 season, he played 41 league games for Sunderland and was an outstanding performer in the heart of the Roker defence as Peter Reid's team lifted the First Division title and won promotion to the Premier League.

Dickie went on to make over 280 appearances for the club, before a move to Queens Park Rangers in 1998 brought his Sunderland career to a close. Sadly, a serious knee injury sustained in the first few minutes of his Rangers debut in a pre-season friendly brought down the curtain on Dickie's top-class career. Still living in the North East, Dickie had a spell managing Durham City before resigning in October 2012.

"A big, strong, powerful centre-back who could also play at left-back, Dickie joined Sunderland in 1986 straight from school.

"His robust style of play and never-say-die approach made him a great favourite with the fans who would regularly chant 'Who needs Cantona when we've got Dickie Ord' from the Roker Park terraces!"

Micky

GARY OWERS

Born in Gateshead, Gary Owers was a star player with Chester-le-Street Schoolboys before joining Sunderland as a 16-year-old straight from school. Gary was handed his first-team debut by Denis Smith during Sunderland's solitary season in English football's third tier and made 37 appearances in a campaign that saw the club lift the Third Division title.

A fiercely competitive player with pace and energy, Gary was employed predominantly as a midfielder, but was equally at home in the full-back position. A role he performed admirably, particularly when he stood in for the suspended Paul Hardyman in the 1990 Division One Play-Off semi-final second leg against Newcastle United at St James' Park.

On a great night for Sunderland Football Club, Gary set up the opening goal for Eric Gates in a truly memorable 2-0 victory to clinch a place at Wembley. Two years later, he was back at Wembley again, this time in the FA Cup final against Liverpool and again in the full-back role, on this occasion standing in for the injured John Kay.

Gary's Roker Park career spanned almost ten years during which he made over 300 appearances before joining Bristol City midway through the 1994/95 season. He then joined Notts County before moving into non-league football and eventually management. Most recently, in June 2015, Gary was appointed assistant manager to his old Sunderland boss Malcolm Crosby at Conference club Gateshead.

"Gary was an all-action type of player who gave everything for the shirt in every game.

"He was a box-to-box player who would never let you down and if the opposition had a player who was a little dangerous, Gary would be the one to sort him out."
Micky

KEVIN PHILLIPS

When Sunderland manager Peter Reid clinched the signing of Kevin Phillips during the 1997 close-season, few Sunderland fans had even heard of the young Watford forward, yet within a few short years the Hitchin-born striker had achieved legendary status on Wearside.

Kevin exploded onto the scene when he scored on his Sunderland debut in a 3-1 victory over Manchester City in the Stadium of Light's first-ever competitive game and, after quickly forming a devastating striking partnership with Niall Quinn, Kevin finished the campaign with 35 league and cup goals.

Whilst the season ended in major disappointment after losing to Charlton Athletic in the Division One Play-Off final at Wembley, Kevin had entered the record books, becoming the first player since Brian Clough to break the 30 goal barrier.

The following season saw Sunderland clinch promotion in style, lifting the Division One title with a record 105 points. An injury sustained early in the campaign restricted Kevin's league appearances to just 26, yet he still finished the campaign as the club's top striker with 23 goals. To cap a great season, Kevin won his first full international cap for England when he played in a friendly international against Hungary in Budapest, the first of his eight caps for his country, all won during his time with Sunderland.

However, even better was to follow in the 1999/2000 season, undoubtedly the finest of Kevin's career on Wearside, as he picked up the coveted Golden Boot award after finishing as European football's top scorer with 30 Premier League goals. After securing two seventh place finishes, Sunderland appeared to have finally become established in English football's top flight, but in the seasons that followed their form dipped badly culminating in relegation at the end of the 2002/03 season.

Due to the financial constraints of the lower division, the club were forced to sell many of their star players and it came as no surprise when Kevin brought the curtain down on a truly brilliant Sunderland career by joining Southampton in a £3.25 million transfer. He then enjoyed spells in the Midlands with Aston Villa, West Bromwich Albion and Birmingham City before joining Blackpool during the 2011 close-season. Kevin then played for Crystal Palace and Leicester City before finally hanging up his boots at the end of the 2013/14 season at the age of 41.

"Probably the best value for money signing Sunderland have ever made, we signed Kevin from Watford for just £325,000 - what a bargain! Kevin went on to score 130 goals for Sunderland, usually alongside Niall Quinn, which was such a great combination.

"We would get crosses in and around the box and Niall would head them down for Kevin, who would invariably be nearby, to pick the ball up and knock it in! Kevin did so well, he eventually got an England call-up and whilst he went on to play eight games for his country - it really should have been more. A legend with the Sunderland fans who will never forget him, Kevin is now first-team coach at Derby County."

Micky

NICK PICKERING

South Shields-born, Nick Pickering signed schoolboy terms with Sunderland in September 1977 and was capped by England at youth international level as he progressed through the ranks at Roker Park. He made his first-team debut when he played in a 3-3 draw against Ipswich Town on the opening day of the 1981/82 season alongside other Sunderland debutants Ally McCoist and Iain Munro.

Nick made 37 appearances during that first campaign and was voted both Young Player of the Year and Player of the Year by supporters. He hardly missed a game in the four years that followed and was an ever-present in the 1983/84 season, a campaign during which he moved to the left-back position alongside Barry Venison on the opposite flank.

Nick's outstanding form led to international recognition when he was capped by England at Under-21 level and he was part of the squad that lifted the European Championship in 1984. Nick also won a full international cap for his country when he played against Australia in Melbourne in June 1983.

Nick's Sunderland career came to a close in January 1986, when he joined Coventry City in a £125,000 deal, but he signed off in style by netting a memorable hat-trick against Leeds United in his penultimate game at Roker Park. At Coventry, Nick enjoyed great success, helping the Sky Blues win the FA Cup for the first time ever in 1987 with a 3-2 victory over Tottenham Hotspur at Wembley. The following year he moved to Derby County and then played for Darlington and Burnley before retiring from the game in June 1994.

After his playing days were over, Nick returned to the North East and moved into coaching, working predominantly with youngsters, as well as becoming involved in media work with local radio.

"Nick was one of the few players capped by England at full international level whilst playing for Sunderland.

"He was a local lad who came through the ranks at Roker Park and went on to enjoy a great career as a professional footballer. A left-sided player who could operate either at full-back or midfield, Nick was a tall, classy player with an excellent left foot."

Micky

RITCHIE PITT

Ritchie Pitt graduated through the ranks at Roker Park and was a member of Sunderland's 1969 FA Youth Cup-winning team, a season that also saw him make his league debut at the age of only 17. A tall and skilful central defender, he had already been capped by England at Under-15 and Under-18 level and when Sunderland reached the FA Cup final in 1973, Ritchie was the only member of the Sunderland squad to have previously played at Wembley.

Amazingly, he may not have tasted the glory of the cup win, having been placed on the transfer list shortly after Bob Stokoe's arrival at Roker Park in November 1972 and it was only after an injury to David Young that Ritchie found himself recalled to the Roker rear-guard.

Once back in the side however, he was able to show his true worth, producing some heroic performances alongside Dave Watson in the heart of the Sunderland defence for the remainder of the cup run, not least in the final itself when he produced arguably his greatest display in a Sunderland shirt.

The future certainly looked bright for the Seaham-born defender, but only a few games into the following campaign he sustained a knee injury that brought his relatively short career to an end. Having been forced to retire from the game, Ritchie went into teaching and after working in the Channel Islands, he returned to the North East as Head of Year at Seaham Comprehensive School.

"A big strong centre-back, who was great in the air and only used his right foot to stand on, Ritchie loved the challenge of marking a centre-forward. In the '73 final, he made a slightly late tackle on Allan Clarke in the first few minutes (he always says he got there as quickly as he could!) and that set the tone for the rest of the game.

"It made the rest of us realise we had to be at our best and give everything to win this game. He was very competitive and still is - we play golf and snooker together every week, only for a pound

IAN PORTERFIELD

As long as football is played on Wearside, Ian Porterfield's 1973 FA Cup-winning goal will remain one of the most iconic moments of the club's history. Ironically, the man who scored what is widely regarded as the most famous goal ever scored by a Sunderland player was never normally renowned for his goalscoring prowess.

Bought from Raith Rovers for £30,000 in December 1967, Ian was seen by the Roker Park management as the man to replace the legendary Jim Baxter following the Scottish international's departure to Nottingham Forest.

After making his debut in the red-hot atmosphere of a Tyne-Wear derby at Roker Park, Ian soon became a first-team regular and for the best part of eight years he was the engine-room of the Sunderland midfield. However, his football career almost came to an abrupt end in December 1974 when he sustained serious head injuries following a horrific car crash and only the expertise of the surgeons at Newcastle General Hospital saved his life.

After battling back to fitness, he eventually joined Sheffield Wednesday as player-coach and soon afterwards began a long and successful career in football management both at club and international level. When he died in September 2007 at the age of 61, he was still in charge of the Armenian national team and had just recorded a memorable 1-1 draw against Portugal in a European Championship qualifier in Yerevan.

"Sadly no longer with us, Ian was the brains of our team. A skilful, elegant player with a beautiful left foot, he glided across the pitch giving us the platform to go forward and keep possession.

"Of course, Ian will be remembered for scoring the winner in the final, and with his right foot, something he never used! I remember him always talking about football, all day and every day. Just after I got into the first team we used to go to a cafe for lunch and if you were on same table as Ian, he would give you earache talking football. One day I was sat with him and he said 'Can I give you some advice, we love having you in the team, winning the ball for us and giving us all your energy, but can I say, when you win the ball, give it to one of us who can play (which I thought I could) and don't try and do too much.' I followed Ian's advice for the rest of my career. Ian was a lovely guy and is a massive miss."

Micky

NIALL QUINN

One of the greatest figures in the history of Sunderland Football Club, Niall Quinn will always be a legend on Wearside. Signed from Manchester City by Peter Reid in August 1996, Niall was almost 30 years of age when he arrived at Roker Park, yet was about to embark on what would turn out to be probably the finest period of a career that had begun with Arsenal 13 years earlier.

However, the big Irishman could hardly have got off to a worse start with his new club, when a serious knee ligament injury sustained in a game against Coventry City kept him out of the side for the best part of a season that saw Sunderland relegated to Division One.

The following campaign saw Sunderland begin life at the Stadium of Light and Niall entered the record books when he scored the club's first-ever goal at their new home after netting the opening goal in a 3-1 victory over Manchester City. Also on the score-sheet that night was new signing Kevin Phillips and soon, the Quinn-Phillips partnership would take the league by storm, with Niall's aerial dominance providing the perfect foil for SuperKev's goalscoring prowess.

After losing to Charlton Athletic in the Play-Off final at Wembley at the end of the 1997/98 season, Sunderland were dominant in the league the following campaign, lifting the Division One title with the Quinn-Phillips partnership contributing 41 of the club's 91 goals. For a few seasons the pair were unstoppable and probably the best striking partnership in the Premier League, but by 2003, the club had slipped back into Division Two. Niall made only eight appearances during the relegation season before a troublesome back injury brought his playing days to an end.

During a glorious career, Niall won 92 caps for the Republic of Ireland, who fittingly provided the opposition for his testimonial at the Stadium of Light in 2002, the proceeds from which he generously donated to local charities.

"A centre-forward who played for Arsenal and Man City, Niall came to us near the end of his career, but because of the team and the formation we played at the time, Sunderland probably got more out of Niall than his previous clubs ever did. He scored lots of goals as well as providing countless assists for SuperKev, and he even went in goal for us on one occasion!

"After his playing days were over Niall came back to Sunderland to rescue the club and even took over as manager until he found the right person, although I think he will admit that he was not too successful in that particular job! He then went on to become our chairman and did a great job firstly persuading the Drumaville Consortium to come in and take over from Sir Bob Murray, then bringing Ellis Short on board to hopefully take us to the next level. Niall is a true gentleman, great company and we will always love him for what he has done for Sunderland both on and off the pitch."

Micky

BRYAN ROBSON

Bryan 'Pop' Robson was born literally within a stone's throw of Roker Park, yet amazingly, Sunderland missed out on signing the youngster who went on to become one of the finest strikers in the history of North East football. Instead, young Bryan was picked up by arch-rivals Newcastle United, where he eventually became something of a legend on Tyneside, particularly after his goals helped win the Inter-Cities Fairs in 1969.

Two years later, Pop joined West Ham United in a £120,000 transfer and in the 1972/73 season he finished as the Football League's top scorer with 28 goals. In 1974 however, he returned to the North East to join Sunderland, the team he had supported as a youngster, and was leading scorer in his first two seasons at Roker Park.

In the 1975/76 season his goals helped his club clinch the Second Division title, but early in the following campaign he rejoined the Hammers, only to return to Roker three years later. Again, Pop joined a promotion campaign with Sunderland having slipped back into Division Two and again, he finished as top scorer with 20 league goals as the club regained their place in the top flight, finishing as runners-up to Leicester City.

Pop then joined Carlisle United as player-coach and held a similar post with Chelsea before returning for a third spell with Sunderland at the age of almost 38. However, he quickly proved he had lost none of his sharpness in front of goal when he netted after only six minutes in his debut against West Bromwich Albion at Roker Park. Pop's final appearance in a Sunderland shirt came at Leicester on the final day of the 1983/84 season when, at the age of 38 years and 182 days. he became the oldest player ever to score in a competitive game for Sunderland.

After finally hanging up his boots, Pop went on to enjoy a lengthy career in coaching, serving Sunderland in various roles and also working for Sir Alex Ferguson at Manchester United.

"Regarded in the game by his fellow professionals as the best forward never to play for England, Pop was a great striker, not particularly big but very fit, quick and agile.

"He scored all kinds of different goals, from tap-ins to spectacular volleys and headers. Pop was a great professional and would cost an absolute fortune if he was around today. After retiring from the game he quickly earned a reputation as an excellent coach and until recently, he was Sunderland's chief scout."

Micky

DANNY ROSE

Although Danny Rose spent only a single season with Sunderland, his performances throughout his time at the Stadium of Light made him a hugely popular player with Sunderland fans who voted him their Young Player of the Year at the end of the campaign.

Signed by Martin O'Neill on a season-long loan from Tottenham Hotspur on 31 August 2012, the Leeds-born full-back had already been capped by England at Under-17, Under-19 and Under-21 levels and made his Sunderland debut against Liverpool at the Stadium of Light shortly after arriving on Wearside.

A full-back with real pace, Danny made an instant impact with supporters who immediately warmed to his skilful, surging runs down the left flank and his ability to consistently deliver accurate crosses into the box.

Danny scored his first goal for Sunderland in a Premier League fixture against Aston Villa at Villa Park, a brilliant strike that had Sunderland's new manager Paolo Di Canio signing the full-back's praises. For the remainder of the season he was a key figure in Sunderland's ultimately successful survival bid and played his final game for the club in their 1-1 draw with Southampton at the Stadium of Light with supporters giving him a rousing reception at the final whistle.

"Maybe another surprise in my top fifty, but I had to have Danny in there, as I think he is a player of the highest quality and one of the best full-backs that we have seen at our club in recent times.

"Danny was only with us on a season-long loan from Tottenham, but he showed us just the type of player you need to survive in the Premier League. A modern day left-back, Danny is blessed with a lot of pace and loves to attack, but unlike most full-backs now, he also wants to defend. He was a massive hit with our supporters because of his winning mentality, willingness to both stop the opposition from scoring and then creating chances for us. Simply one of the best we have had - pity we could not have kept him!"

Micky

GARY ROWELL

A true legend from Sunderland's Roker Park days, Gary Rowell went into the record books when he became Sunderland's joint top post-war goalscorer, equalling the record of 100 goals set by another Roker legend, Len Shackleton.

A local lad and a Sunderland fanatic as a boy, Gary was one of a production line of talented youngsters taken to Roker Park by Sunderland's legendary chief scout Charlie Ferguson. Gary was only 18 when made his first-team debut, coming off the bench in 1-0 victory over Oxford United at Roker Park during Sunderland's Second Division championship-winning season of 1975/76.

In those early days of his career, Gary was used predominantly in midfield and it was only when he was used in a more attacking role that his career began to flourish. In 1977/78 he netted 18 goals in 38 appearances and faired even better the following campaign when he found the net 21 times including a truly memorable hat-trick in a 4-1 victory over Newcastle United at St James' Park. It was Gary's first-ever hat-trick for Sunderland and of all the goals he scored for the club, none were sweeter than that particular treble, a feat that guaranteed him a place in football folklore on Wearside for all time.

The following season saw Sunderland clinch promotion to Division One, but a medial ligament injury sustained towards the end of the previous campaign restricted Gary's appearances to just eight. However, after regaining fitness he was a regular in the team for the next four years, his clinical finishing, particularly from the penalty spot, continuing to be the feature of his game and older supporters will no doubt recall a memorable treble against Arsenal in December 1982.

Gary's Sunderland career came to a close in August 1984 when he was somewhat surprisingly sold to Norwich City by new manager Len Ashurst. Ironically, the two clubs met in the Milk Cup final later that season and although injury had kept Gary out of the victorious City team, after the final whistle he demonstrated his love of Sunderland by bringing the trophy over to salute the red and white fans packed behind the goal.

"Gary was an apprentice at the time of our cup run in '73 and was one of those kids you knew would one day be a big player for Sunderland, and big he was! He became a cult hero in the area for his goal scoring feats, none more so than when he scored a hat-trick against the old enemy over the water on the 24 February 1979, a date he will never forget.

"Gary had a good football brain and would always be in the right place at the right time, but it was his finishing and his great goals that the supporters loved him for. He went on to score 100 goals for Sunderland, a club record until Kevin Phillips showed up. After his playing days were over Gary became a favourite on the radio, commentating on the Sunderland games."

Micky

NICK SHARKEY

Signed by Sunderland in May 1958, Nick Sharkey demonstrated his goalscoring ability right from the start, netting an amazing 140 goals for the fifth team in his first season on Wearside. In an era when centre-forwards were invariably tall and powerfully built, Nick's lack of inches proved to be no handicap and he went on to become one of Sunderland's finest post-war goalscorers.

He made his first-team debut in a Division Two game against Scunthorpe United in April 1960 but it was not until the 1962/63 season that Nick became established in the Sunderland team chasing promotion to Division One. It was following a serious injury to the team's star centre-forward Brian Clough that Nick got his chance and after that, he was pretty much a regular in the side. Whilst Clough had been a prolific goal-scorer for Sunderland, Nick soon emulated his famous predecessor by equalling a club record after netting five goals in a 7-1 victory against Norwich City at Roker Park.

The season was to end in major disappointment however, when a 1-0 defeat at home to Chelsea on the final day cost Sunderland promotion, although they made it back to the top flight a year later after a marvellous campaign that saw Nick bag 17 league goals. He went one better the following season with 18 in the top division, finishing as the club's leading scorer before eventually losing his place to new signing Neil Martin early in the 1965/66 campaign. A year later, in October 1966, Nick finally severed his ties with the club to join Leicester City in a £15,000 deal. He then enjoyed a spell with Mansfield Town before finishing his career with Hartlepool.

"Sadly, we lost Nick recently - he was a lovely bloke who had time for everyone. Nick was also a great little striker and after making his debut for Sunderland in 1960, he went on to play 99 games for us, scoring 51 goals, an outstanding record for someone so small particularly with all the big hard defenders about in that era.

"Although small he was very tough and had great movement in and around the penalty area where he got most of his goals. A former chairman of our Former Players' Association, Nick is greatly missed."

Micky

THOMAS SORENSEN

Signed for £1 million from Danish club OB Odense during the 1998 close-season, Thomas Sorensen was Sunderland's goalkeeper throughout, what many regard as, the club's finest post-war era. In his first season at the Stadium of Light, Sunderland lifted the First Division title, with Thomas missing only one game and his outstanding performances were a key factor in the club's promotion success.

Tall and powerfully built, yet remarkably agile, Thomas quickly became established as one the Premier League's top 'keepers and in November 1999 he won his first full international cap for Denmark when he came off the bench to replace the injured Peter Schmeichel in a match against Israel. The most memorable moment of his Sunderland career undoubtedly came in November 2000 when he produced a brilliant save from an Alan Shearer penalty late in the game to secure an unforgettable 2-1 victory over Newcastle United at St James' Park.

Sadly, after two seventh place finishes, Peter Reid's team could not maintain their momentum in the top flight and after the club were relegated in 2003, Thomas joined Aston Villa in a £2 million deal. After five seasons at Villa Park he signed for Stoke City and it was during his time at the Britannia Stadium that Thomas announced his retirement from international football after making 101 appearances for his country. His career with Stoke City came to a close at the end of the 2014/15 season and a few months later he headed to Australia to join Melbourne City.

"Thomas is one of the few in my fifty to still be playing. A goalkeeper from Denmark who joined Sunderland in 1998, he became one of the best keepers to play in the Premier League.

"A super-fit and fearless 'keeper, Thomas is a very good shot-stopper and is also excellent on crosses, which is great if you're a defender, watching him come and claim everything."

Micky

COLIN SUGGETT

Born in Washington, Colin was captain of the highly successful Chester-le-Street Boys side that reached the English Schools cup final in 1964 and joined Sunderland straight from school. He went on to star in the club's youth team that lifted the FA Youth Cup in 1966/67, a season during which he also made his first-team debut.

Colin was a striker with pace and exceptional skill and quickly became established as a first-team regular at Roker Park. In his first full campaign, 1967/68, he was an ever-present in the side and also the club's leading scorer with 14 goals. Most notably, he scored in both games against Newcastle United and repeated the feat the following season, quickly becoming something of a thorn in the side of Sunderland's arch-rivals.

The late 60s were a period of struggle for Sunderland and it perhaps came as no surprise when they decided to cash in on their prized asset after receiving a £100,000 bid from West Bromwich Albion, a club record for the Midlands outfit. At the Hawthorns, Colin teamed up alongside England centre-forward Jeff Astle to form one of the most exciting striking partnerships in the top division and enjoyed four seasons with the Baggies before joining Norwich City in February 1973. At Carrow Road, he was deployed in a central midfield role and his outstanding performances earned him the Canaries' Player of the Year award at the end of the 1974/75 season.

In August 1978, Colin returned to the North East to join Newcastle United, before injury brought his career to a close and he moved into coaching, briefly taking over as caretaker-manager at St James' Park, following Willie McFaul's departure in October 1988.

"Colin was a quick player who played just off the main striker. He had a quick brain also and created lots of chances for his colleagues.

"I will always remember Colin for an incident during a practice match. I was a youth player and the manager had us playing a practice match against the first team. Not long into the game a challenge between Colin and I resulted in me coming away with a broken leg - it was a complete accident, but something I will always remember. When his playing days were over, Colin became a very successful coach, having spells at that 'team over the water', Bolton, Portsmouth and Ipswich. These days he is a scout for Norwich City."

Micky

COLIN TODD

Colin Todd was another discovery of Sunderland's chief scout Charlie Ferguson, a man who had brought so many great young players to Roker Park, though few would argue that Colin turned out to be the best of the lot.

Colin had starred in the Chester-le-Street Boys team that reached the English Schools Trophy final in 1964 and within two years, at the age of only 17, he was making his first-team debut for Sunderland alongside the likes of Charlie Hurley, George Herd and Jim Baxter.

The following season he was an ever-present in the side and in the years that followed he rarely missed a game, his outstanding performances in the Roker rear-guard making him one of the hottest properties in the game. Already capped by England at Youth level, Colin won his first Under-23 international cap in May 1968 at the age of only 19.

Early in his Sunderland career, Colin had come under the guidance of Brian Clough who was youth team manager at Roker and it perhaps came as no surprise that when Sunderland decided to sell their star player midway through the 1970/71 season, it was Clough, by now manager of Derby County, who was first in the queue with a cheque for £175,000. At the age of only 22, the move allowed Colin's career to blossom and with the Rams, he enjoyed great success, helping them lift the League title in 1972 and 1975, when he was also named the PFA Player of the Year. In 1972, Colin won his first full international cap for England, eventually going on to play 27 times for his country.

In 1978, Colin joined Everton and later played for Birmingham City before joining up with Brian Clough again at Nottingham Forest. In 1984, he had spells with Oxford United, Luton Town and Vancouver Whitecaps in Canada before hanging up his boots to pursue a career in coaching and management.

"Quite simply one of the two best players I have seen play for Sunderland. Toddy, as we know him, was a fantastic central-defender who had everything needed to play that position - strength, pace, determination and good distribution.

"He loved tackling and defending and although not a big guy, he was also extremely good in the air. Toddy also had a good football brain which helped him read the game and I always thought that when Bobby Moore retired as England captain he was the ready-made replacement, but the people in charge decided to go with other players, like Norman Hunter, who were nowhere near the quality of Toddy."

Micky

DENNIS TUEART

An outstanding talent and a major discovery in the late 1960s, during what was a period of struggle for Sunderland Football Club who seemed to be constantly battling for First Division survival. Dennis made his debut against Sheffield Wednesday on Boxing Day 1968, but after relegation at the end of the following season, it was some years later before his full potential was realised.

Dennis possessed all the qualities of a top-flight left-winger; electric pace, great control and the ability to shoot with both feet and his contribution to SAFC's 1973 FA Cup success cannot be understated. Like most truly great players, he possessed the ability to produce something special and his brilliant solo-effort against Vasas Budapest in Sunderland's first ever European tie together with his overhead scissor-kick volley against Oxford United will live long in the memory of Roker fans.

Having been thrust into the limelight during the 1973 cup run, it came as no surprise when Dennis joined Manchester City less than a year after the Wembley triumph. At Maine Road his career took off in grand style and in the 1976 League Cup final he netted another spectacular overhead strike, this time to clinch a 2-1 win over Newcastle United. Soon afterwards, Dennis won the first of his six full international caps, when he came off the bench to replace Kevin Keegan in England's 1-0 victory over Cyprus in the European Championship in Tsirion, Limassol.

Dennis spent just over four years at Maine Road before heading over the Atlantic to join New York Cosmos where his colleagues included the likes of Franz Beckenbauer and Carlos Alberto. In 1980 he made a sentimental return to Manchester City, which was followed by spells with Stoke City and Burnley before he retired from the game in 1984. Thereafter he has pursued a highly successful business career, although in 1998 he did resume his links with City when he joined the Maine Road board and was later appointed Director of Football.

"Another Newcastle lad, Dennis was a truly great striker. He was skilful, strong, and good in the air for his size and loved taking on full-backs or centre-backs.

"He was also a good goalscorer, so good that he went on to play for England. Dennis and I signed for Manchester City the same day, travelling down together and we made our debut together two days later against Manchester United. Dennis was always so focused and knew what he wanted so he dedicated himself to achieve all he did in the game."

Micky

CHRIS TURNER

Chris Turner's began his career with his local club Sheffield Wednesday where his youth team coach was Ken Knighton and when Knighton took over as Sunderland's manager in 1979 Chris was his first signing, moving to Roker Park in a £100,000 transfer.

He made his Sunderland debut in a 1-1 draw against Ipswich Town early in the 1979/80 season taking over from Barry Siddall and ended up playing 30 games in a campaign that saw Sunderland clinch promotion to Division One. Chris' first season in the top flight was blighted by injuries, firstly a broken jaw sustained against Manchester United and soon afterwards a broken wrist after a collision with Aston Villa's Peter Withe. However, he still managed to produce some brilliant displays, most notably a 'man of the match' performance to deny Manchester United at Old Trafford.

Unfortunately, injuries continued to haunt Chris and in April 1983 he suffered the worst of the lot when he sustained a fractured skull after a shuddering collision with Norwich City's Keith Bertschin. The injury was so severe that initially, there were doubts over Chris' future in the game but in typical fashion, he was back playing again on the opening day of the following season, ironically against Norwich City!

In 1984, Len Ashurst, the man who had handed Chris his debut at Sheffield Wednesday, took over the Roker Park hot-seat and led the club to Wembley in the Milk Cup. Along the way Chris produced some brilliant performances, not least against Tottenham Hotspur at White Hart Lane, when he saved a Graham Roberts penalty to secure a 2-1 victory. Sadly, in the final at Wembley, Chris was beaten by a deflected shot which was enough to give Norwich City a somewhat fortuitous victory. More disappointment was to follow when Sunderland were relegated at the end of the campaign and manager Len Ashurst left the club.

Chris was now regarded as one of the finest goalkeepers in the English game and it came as no surprise when he joined Manchester United during the 1985 close-season in a £275,000 transfer. His career at Old Trafford lasted three seasons before he rejoined Sheffield Wednesday where he enjoyed great success helping them lift the League Cup and clinch promotion to Division One in 1991. Chris later enjoyed spells in management with Leyton Orient and Hartlepool and also held coaching posts with Leicester City and Wolverhampton Wanderers.

"One of a few goalkeepers I have in my fifty, Chris played 224 games for us and although not a big fella as most goalkeepers usually are, he one was of the best I have seen at Sunderland.

"A fearless 'keeper, Chris made up for his lack of inches with his speed around the box, his very fast reactions and his great ability to make instinctive saves."

Micky

BARRY VENISON

One of the finest full-backs to come through the ranks at Roker Park, Barry Venison made his first-team debut at the age of only 17, when he played at Notts County early in the 1981/82 season. Barry stayed in the side for four months after making a great start to his top-level career and will probably be best remembered for a stunning volley when he came off the bench to clinch a 3-2 victory over Manchester City at Maine Road.

Capped by England at youth international level, Barry soon became a permanent fixture in the number two shirt, his competitive, yet skilful style winning plaudits from the Sunderland fans on the terraces. He was made vice-captain at the start of the 1984/85 season and captained the side for the Milk Cup final at Wembley after suspension had cost Shaun Elliott his place in the side. Defeat in the final was followed by relegation and whilst Barry played a full season in Division Two, a move to the bigger stage became inevitable and in July 1986, he joined Liverpool in a £250,000 transfer.

He enjoyed six great seasons at Anfield and was capped twice by England before joining Newcastle United during the summer of 1992. Barry then enjoyed a spell in Turkey with Galatasaray where he linked up with his former Liverpool boss Graeme Souness. He then joined Southampton, but his two years with the south coast club were blighted by injury, forcing him to retire from the game in October 1997. After a spell in media work, Barry moved to America where he became a highly successful property developer before ending his twelve-year break from the game to take over as technical director of Orange County Blues FC in California.

"A local lad who actually comes from the same town as myself, Barry was an excellent full-back who had lots of class, a bit of pace and could also read the game.

"He became captain whilst still quite young and became such a good player that Liverpool came in and took him to Anfield, where he had a great career. He was captain of our Milk Cup team in 1985 and now lives in America where I'm sure he will be making an impression with his dress sense!"

Micky

DAVE WATSON

When Dave Watson arrived at Roker Park in December 1970, little was known of the club's new £100,000 signing from Rotherham United, yet it soon became apparent that, just as he had done with the capture of Charlie Hurley from Millwall 13 years earlier, Sunderland boss Alan Brown had unearthed another gem from the lower leagues. Both players were inspired signings by Brown and each went on to become arguably the finest central-defenders of their generation.

Ironically however, it was as a centre-forward that Brown first used Watson and it was only following the arrival of Bob Stokoe as manager that the Nottingham-born player reverted to his more accustomed role of centre-half. Sunderland's marvellous FA Cup run in 1973 was the catalyst for Dave's career and his Man of the Match performance against Leeds United in the final was soon followed by full international honours when he was capped for England in a friendly international against Portugal in April 1974.

With Sunderland failing to secure promotion in the two seasons following their cup triumph, it came as no surprise when Sunderland's star defender was chased by a posse of top clubs, with Manchester City eventually persuading Watson to join his former Roker Park colleagues Dennis Tueart and Micky Horswill at Maine Road. Having won 14 caps during his time at Roker Park, Dave had become Sunderland's most-capped England international and he would go on to appear no less than 65 times for his country.

In a wonderful career spanning almost two decades, Dave also played for Southampton, Stoke City and Derby County as well as having spells abroad with German side Werder Bremen and Vancouver Whitecaps in Canada.

"Dave came to us from Rotherham United as a centre-forward, but after a while he was moved to centre-back and became in my opinion, the best Sunderland ever had, even better than the King, Mr Hurley.

"Dave was so good both in the air and on the ground that he never missed a header and his timing when tackling was second to none. In my view, he was our best player in the cup final and certainly the finest I ever played with defensively. There's no question that even in today's game, Dave would be still one of the best around."

Micky

BILLY WHITEHURST

One of the toughest characters in the game during the 1980s and 90s, Billy Whitehurst began his career in non-league football while still working as a bricklayer. Billy's move into the big time came in 1980 when Hull City paid Midland League club Mexborough Town £2,500 for his services, to begin a career in league football that would see him serve no fewer than nine different clubs.

At Boothferry Park, Billy quickly earned a reputation as a rugged centre-forward who took no prisoners, but the big striker also had an eye for goal, which soon attracted the attention of a number of top clubs and in December 1985, Newcastle United paid £232,000 for his services. His stay at St James' Park lasted less than twelve months, but after spells with Oxford United and Reading, Billy returned to the North East to join Sunderland.

He made his debut in a 3-2 defeat at Birmingham shortly after the start of the 1988/89 season and scored his first goal for the club in a 2-1 victory over Leeds United at Roker Park. Bought by manager Denis Smith to play alongside Marco Gabbiadini, Billy stayed in the side for three months, but when the partnership failed to develop he was sold to Hull City. Three months later he returned to Roker Park with the Tigers and in typical fashion was sent off after a clash with John McPhail.

Thereafter, Billy had a procession of clubs, rarely staying very long at any and after retiring from the game in 1994, he took over the Cricketer's Arms, a pub adjacent to Sheffield United's Bramall Lane ground.

"And finally Billy Whitehurst and before you start scratching your heads at that choice, there is method in my madness. The players featured in the preceding pages all had great qualities as professional footballers – skill, pace, vision and all-round ability. Well, Billy had none of these!

...but he was, without doubt, the hardest player I ever came across during my time watching Sunderland - forget Tommy Smith, Chopper Harris or Wimbledon's Crazy Gang, none of these could match Billy Whitehurst. I've also included him because, quite simply, if I didn't, I would probably get the biggest thumping ever! A great friend of mine, I love him!"

Micky